TOM HEIL

# Made for War

*A Blueprint for Spiritual Warfare*

*Copyright © 2025 by Tom Heil*

*All rights reserved. No part of this publication may be reproduced, stored or transmitted in any form or by any means, electronic, mechanical, photocopying, recording, scanning, or otherwise without written permission from the publisher. It is illegal to copy this book, post it to a website, or distribute it by any other means without permission.*

*Scripture Quotations:*

*Unless otherwise noted, all Scripture quotations are taken from The Modern English Version of the Holy Bible. Copyright © 2014 by Military Bible Association. Used by permission. All rights reserved. Published and distributed by Charisma House.*

*First edition*

*ISBN: 979-8-9920737-0-6*

*Editing by Alisha Heil*
*Editing by Jacqueline Kurceba*

*This book was professionally typeset on Reedsy.*
*Find out more at reedsy.com*

*This book is dedicated to those whose purpose may be ignited by its message. Remember, God has a plan for you, and you are Made for War!*

# Contents

*Foreword* — iii
*Acknowledgments* — v
Introduction — 1
1  Made for War — 3
2  Removing Legal Rights from the Enemy — 13
  Legal Rights — 14
    Unforgiveness — 14
    Secrets/Lies — 16
    Soul Ties — 18
    Demonic Agreements & Occultism — 21
3  A Spiritual War — 26
  Given Authority in the Battlefield and the Courts of Heaven — 29
    Soldiers — 29
    Judicial Enforcer — 31
      Defense Attorney — 32
      Prosecuting Attorney — 34
      Court Room Witness — 36
4  Armed & Dangerous — 39
  Use The Word as a Weapon! — 39
  Our Weapons Are Not Carnal — 42
  Types of Weapons — 43
    Prayer — 44
    Fasting — 47

|   |   |
|---|---|
| Prophecy | 49 |
| Calling in Reinforcements | 51 |
| Armor of God | 54 |
| Worship | 57 |
| 5 An Inheritance of Victory | 60 |
| From Generational Curses to Generational Blessings | 65 |
| It's Time to Change your Posture. | 68 |
| Final Revelation | 73 |

# Foreword

In **I Timothy 1:18**, the Apostle Paul urges his young son in the ministry to **wage a good warfare**, especially concerning the prophecies he had received. The Greek word for "warfare" is **strateía** (*strat-i'-ah*), meaning an expedition, a military campaign, or service accompanied by difficulties that oppose us and interfere with our Christian journey of serving God.

Jesus confirms this warfare in the last verse of **John 16**, where He reveals that during our lifetime in this world, we will face trouble, trials, suffering, distress, persecution, oppression, afflictions, sorrows, and tribulations. Yet, He also tells us to **be of good cheer**, for He has **victoriously overcome the world**! And because Jesus has overcome, we can too!

In this book, **"Made For War,"** my spiritual son, **Pastor Tom Heil, Jr.,** has created a blueprint that anyone can read, follow, and apply. As you delve into the pages of this manual, prepare to be enlightened, empowered, strengthened, and—most importantly—**mentally transformed and equipped** for any battle with the kingdom of darkness.

**Read, absorb, learn, apply, and wage a good warfare!**

**Dr. Rodderick Jenerette**

**Senior Leader**
**Next Jeneration Apostolic Network**

# Acknowledgments

First, I would like to thank the Lord, for the Holy Spirit has truly inspired this work. Beyond any individual, I would like to give honor and thanks to my wife. Without her love and support, I would not be here today. Lastly, to everyone who has contributed to this process, both directly and indirectly, your love, prayers, and support have made this possible. I am truly blessed.

# Introduction

As I reviewed the nearly finished product of this book, a question came to mind: Why would someone want to read this book? This led me to reflect on my past experiences as a deliverance minister and a trainer of the body of Christ. I have noticed that many people desire supernatural encounters in their faith journey, but they are often held back by fear of the unknown. This fear acts as a barrier, preventing them from fully embracing the potential of such experiences.

However, we must remember that our protection ultimately comes from Christ and the authority we have been given. Unfortunately, both the body of Christ and society as a whole have been influenced, targeted, and deceived into adopting Hollywood's distorted portrayal of deliverance and spiritual warfare. This has instilled a paralyzing fear in many individuals. Additionally, flawed church leadership and doctrine have led people to believe that they should avoid confronting the forces of darkness at all costs, which is far from the truth. This book can be incredibly valuable for believers because it can help those who have been trapped in fear to take a step forward towards embracing the victory that is already theirs through Christ.

As the reader, you will not only receive a blueprint for spiritual warfare but also be empowered to handle situations involving deliverance and spiritual warfare that others may shy away from. This book will help you understand that you are "made for war" and fully equipped to confront the forces of darkness that seek to influence, manipulate, and even destroy your life and the calling that God has placed on you. It is noteworthy that spiritual warfare is one of the most searched topics among Christians, yet it is often something that churches avoid equipping their members for completely.

When engaging in deliverance ministry, whether through teaching or personal sessions, I do not approach calling out demons or breaking curses from a stance of intimidation. Instead, I operate from a position of knowing that I am "made for war" and have been trained and equipped for spiritual battle. The enemy's tactics of intimidation, whether through ignorance about spiritual warfare or a lack of intentional equipping by some churches, must come to an end. God is raising up a remnant who can confidently confront the forces of darkness and uphold the kingdom of light. This group of individuals is ready to advocate for their fellow believers in every area where the enemy has waged warfare. It is time to no longer be passive recipients of spiritual warfare, but to thrive in the midst of it with excellence. Let us embrace the blueprint, acknowledge that we are "made for war," and step into the victory that God has already prepared for us.

# 1

# Made for War

*Blessed be the Lord my strength, who prepares my hands for war, and my fingers to fight*

Psalms 144:1

Spiritual warfare is one of the most searched topics in the Christian community, regardless of denomination or region. It holds a constant fascination for the body of Christ. What if I told you that this is because we are made for a spiritual battle? Not that our sole purpose is war, but rather that we are equipped and built with the capacity to engage in it as sons and daughters of God. Within the realm of being Believers in Jesus, we are equipped to do the Lord's will on Earth. A crucial starting point is recognizing that our strength comes from the Lord. This understanding is essential, as we will discuss later. The Psalmist who wrote Psalm 144:1 begins by acknowledging the source of his strength, stating that his hands have been prepared for war and his fingers for combat. The preparation of your hands by God equips and arms you for your Divine assignment. Imagine how many individuals in the church would passionately and boldly pursue God's purpose if they were aware that their hands and fingers had been prepared for it.

The connection to spiritual warfare lies in the fact that we have been equipped in a manner that places the enemy under our feet. Our approach to battle is not that of individuals striving to overcome a superior foe, but rather as victors engaging the enemy who is already positioned beneath our feet. We engage in combat with the knowledge that "no weapon formed against you shall prosper" (Isaiah 54:17), that the "gates of hell will not prevail" (Matthew 16:18, KJV), and that we will "resist the devil, and he will flee from you" (James 4:7). All of this is achievable through our submission to God and our identity as sons and daughters of the Most High.

Our promises, which serve as divine advantages and grant us divine authority, emanate from God. He prepares us for spiritual battle. This doesn't necessarily imply that a warlike mentality should always prevail, but rather underscores our constant state of preparedness. The necessary attributes are already within us, accessible through obedience and our relationship with the Lord.

A prevalent issue is that many people have become overly occupied with promoting themselves and trying to pray their way out of the preparation that God has already anointed them for in the context of warfare. While it's true that God desires our prosperity and wants us to experience joy and peace that surpasses all understanding, the reality is that we often pursue these things with selfish motives. Warfare is not a concept to fear or avoid; rather, it's something we step into with the assurance that we are already equipped for it and that God has already supplied everything we need.

David's boldness and confidence in preparing to face Goliath, as described in 1 Samuel 17, exemplify this principle of preparation. He selected stones that were readily available and used a sling he already possessed. Saul's armor didn't suit him, but what David had was sufficient. He recognized that God had already provided all that he needed.

*He trains my hands for war, so that my arms bend a bow of bronze.*
Psalms 18:34

God's preparation doesn't rely solely on what's already within us. There are things we have not yet grasped that we need to be trained for, and blueprints for warfare that need to be attained and understood. He also trains us for what lies ahead. As we submit to God and lead consecrated lives, we can attune ourselves to His voice and grasp His plans for us, understanding His guidance within each season. Studying His scriptures further deepens our comprehension of living righteously and engaging in battle. Through His Word and our connection with Christ, in partnership with the Holy Spirit, we undergo the training necessary to become the warriors God intends us to be.

Reflecting on Psalm 18:34 is genuinely empowering. It speaks of God training our hands for war and enabling our arms to bend a bow of bronze. The use of bronze as a metaphorical material highlights the immense power God aims to instill in us—the authority and might He desires to work within and through us. Bending bronze might be beyond human capability, yet we know we have access to supernatural strength and power through our faith.

Comprehending this verse has the potential to greatly empower believers. Understanding the challenge of bending a bow made of bronze reinforces the teachings that Jesus has already imparted to us as Christians. Jesus proclaimed that if we possess faith even as small as a mustard seed, nothing would be beyond our reach (Matthew 17:20). The notion of having sufficient faith to step into the realm of the impossible aligns with the kind of unwavering belief that can empower us to accomplish feats like bending a bow of bronze. This achievement doesn't stem from our own strength but from His divine training of our hands.

We understand that God not only readies our hands and provides us with all the necessary tools for spiritual warfare, but He also imparts training to our hands. Consequently, as we heed God's voice in obedience, the unattainable becomes attainable. It's crucial to remember that upon becoming children of God, we are transformed into supernatural beings, for we are no longer citizens of Earth but citizens of heaven (Ephesians 2:19-22).

In this era of Apostolic Reformation, becoming aware of our authority and capabilities in spiritual warfare is essential for the body of Christ. In other words, comprehending not only what we are called to do but also how we are called to do it provides us with clarity in our purpose and direction. For instance, just as a scientist undergoes schooling to grasp various facets of science, enabling them to function effectively in their field, as believers, it is our responsibility to not only diligently study and show ourselves approved but also to receive training and guidance from the Lord to effectively carry out our calling.

This is not a time for passive Christianity, where we sit on the sidelines during the battle. Instead, it is a time to actively engage in the fight, utilizing the equipping we have already received. As believers, we are designated as warriors, authoritative voices, and representatives of the kingdom here on Earth—akin to officials and ambassadors. We will delve into these aspects further in our discussion.

Contrary to commonly preached beliefs, our role extends beyond being mere warriors slogging through the battlefield. Instead, we engage in battle from a position of victory. Our authority doesn't derive from a lower standing; it emanates from a place of governance. Rather than being soldiers crawling through the mud on the battlefield, we embody the role of ambassadors with privileged access to the courts of heaven. We are more akin to those called to governance, seated in elevated positions within Christ (Ephesians 2:6).

> *Put on the whole armor of God that you may be able to stand against the schemes of the devil. For our fight is not against flesh and blood, but against principalities, against powers, against the rulers of the darkness of this world, and against spiritual forces of evil in the heavenly places. Therefore, take up the whole armor of God that you may be able to resist in the evil day, and having done all, to stand. Stand therefore, having your waist girded with truth,*

*having put on the breastplate of righteousness, having your feet fitted with the readiness of the gospel of peace, and above all, taking the shield of faith, with which you will be able to extinguish all the fiery arrows of the evil one. Take the helmet of salvation and the sword of the Spirit, which is the word of God.*
Ephesians 6:11-17

Allow me to pose a question: Why would God provide armor to His people if we weren't destined for warfare? Reflect on this—what purpose would it serve for God's people to possess armor if there were no battle or conflict to confront? Regrettably, many individuals tend to interpret this metaphorically, overlooking the fact that armor is typically granted during times of battle.

The scripture begins by identifying the nature of our struggle; it emphasizes that our battle isn't against flesh and blood. This understanding can bring clarity and offer insight into various situations where people often find themselves in distress. For instance, it can salvage marriages by reminding couples that their conflict isn't against each other but rather alongside each other. Similarly, the battles we face aren't against our neighbors or relatives; instead, we should be fighting alongside or for them. It's crucial to realize that there are darker spiritual forces at play which we are called to combat, and God has bestowed upon us the necessary equipment for this purpose.

The scripture in Ephesians 6:11-17 enumerates the various components of the armor of God. Each of these elements is significant in attaining victory in spiritual warfare. Being equipped with the appropriate armor instills confidence and enabling effective combat against opposing forces. For example, the scripture emphasizes that our waist is to be girded with truth. As believers, we are tasked with living in truth, for the scriptures also affirm that the truth will set us free (John 8:32).

The verse also highlights the significance of the breastplate of righteousness. This prompts us to ask: What exactly is a breastplate? A breastplate is a piece of armor designed to shield the chest, where the heart is located. As believers, it is crucial to safeguard our hearts—a principle rooted in the Bible. Proverbs 4:23 which declares "Keep your heart will all diligence, for out of it are the issues in life" underscores the importance of guarding our hearts, offering a profound directive.

Righteousness serves as a protective barrier for the believer. As we diligently pursue righteousness and align ourselves with His standards, we elevate our way of life beyond worldly norms. In doing so, we adopt a posture that safeguards us against the enemy's assaults. This approach involves fortifying ourselves with His word and embracing the way He has called us to live.

*But whoever listens to me will dwell safely, and will be secure from fear of evil.*
Proverbs 1:33

At the heart of righteousness lies obedience—adhering to the will of God. As we grasp this concept and position ourselves in alignment with His obedience and righteousness, we open ourselves to a heightened level of heart protection that we may not have encountered before.

The scripture in Ephesians 6:15 instructs us to have our feet fitted with the gospel of peace. This symbolizes our manner of walking and underscores the importance of guarding our path; therefore, every step we take should be guided by Christ and immersed in His peace. This principle applies not only to how we conduct ourselves in our personal lives but also to how we interact with and perceive others. The gospel of peace should serve as a guiding principle that shapes our actions and operations as believers. Furthermore, in our spiritual warfare, the gospel of grace transforms our approach. In this era of grace, we no longer engage in combat by hurling curses at our adversaries; instead, we approach with a lens of love and peace, systematically dismantling malevolent forces. This approach embodies the love and peace that Christ has called us to embrace and exemplify in our walk.

Arguably the most prominent imagery of spiritual warfare within the Ephesians 6:11-17 revolves around the concept of the shield of faith. The scripture states, "the shield of faith, with which you will be able to extinguish all the fiery arrow of the evil one." This imagery of fiery arrows pertains to the tactics and assaults launched by the enemy against our lives as a whole. The adversary deploys supernatural fiery arrows that manifest as attacks. Yet, the verse assures us that our shield of faith possesses the capability to extinguish each one.

Historically, shields in battle served as vital tools to deflect adversary strikes, whether from swords or arrows. Our faith functions similarly—it acts as a safeguard, not only in shielding us, but also safeguarding our priorities and endeavors. A revelation that God showed me about this particular piece of armor was the realization that a shield demands action; it requires being picked up and wielded. Similarly, God urges us to not merely possess faith for defensive purposes but to actively employ it against the enemy. By doing so, we can thwart each assault and fiery arrow directed at our lives and well-being.

The helmet of salvation, arguably one of the most crucial components in a warrior's inventory, safeguards the head and mind. Scripture tells us that we have been given a spirit of love, power, and a sound mind, rather than one of fear (2 Timothy 1:7). The helmet of salvation significantly contributes to our assurance and mental soundness. This concept of salvation is also referenced in Isaiah 59:17, further emphasizing its importance within our repertoire as believers. Its significance is underscored in 1 Thessalonians 5:8, which unequivocally designates the helmet as a paramount protective element in a believer's arsenal. When we allow our salvation and its underlying principles to govern us by living in the fullness thereof, our mindsets can be transformed, resulting in protection through its inherent nature.

The sword of the Spirit, distinct from the other pieces of armor yet still serving a protective purpose, is unequivocally recognized as a weapon. It is explicitly identified as the word of God. This understanding emphasizes that the word of God has a dual role: it serves not only as a defense against the evil one's assaults but also as a means to attack the dominion of darkness with the formidable truth and power of the gospel. Within its pages lie promises capable of dismantling every falsehood, while the power of faith can conquer every shred of fear and doubt. Recognize that your sword is not a mere implement, but a force capable of obliterating any malevolent weapon. If the word assures you that no weapon formed against you shall prosper (Isaiah 54:17), you stand fortified against the adversary's lies and attacks.

Moreover, the word of God is a dynamic force, a two-edged sword that pierces the division between soul and spirit, joints and marrow. It discerns the thoughts and intentions of the heart (Hebrews 4:12). This verse from Hebrews reveals that the word of God is alive and active, signifying that the sword of the Spirit is not a static, two-dimensional tool like other books or weapons. Rather, it ignites into a dynamic, three-dimensional force capable of obliterating any obstacle it encounters. It is described as sharper than a two-edged sword, meaning it penetrates two realms simultaneously. This dual penetration occurs not only in the target it confronts but also in the individual wielding it. The word of God has the remarkable ability to prompt self-reflection and personal correction as one contemplates its content. While functioning as a weapon, the word of God simultaneously acts as a transformative tool, chiseling us deeper into the realms of our calling as believers.

As believers, we are inherently designed for warfare—adeptly equipped, bestowed with gifts, and essential for overcoming any challenge the enemy or life may present. There is no longer a need to accept mediocrity or feign ignorance of our chosen and anointed status, destined to emerge victorious in every spiritual battle.

# 2

# Removing Legal Rights from the Enemy

*All of your words are truth.*
*Every one of your righteous ordinances endures forever.*

Psalms 119:160
World English Bible

In matters of the spiritual realm, the courts of heaven oversee and govern everything, with God seated as the ultimate Judge. The role of Judge is just one facet of God's divine nature; He also serves as Creator, Savior, Redeemer, and more. Understanding the spiritual realm requires recognizing the presence of a kingdom constitution within the Scriptures. These sacred texts not only contain powerful teachings but also possess the status of a binding legal document that commands obedience from all creation.

While we've previously discussed the power and protection

available to us as believers, we often fail to realize that many of our vulnerabilities to the enemy stem from our own actions and lack of knowledge, as illuminated through Scripture. Neglecting essential aspects, such as the impact of unforgiveness, can weaken our defenses and allow the enemy to infiltrate specific areas of our lives. Also, when we are in sin it allows for legal access for the enemy to our lives. In this chapter, we will explore various types of legal rights and discuss their impact on us. We will also delve into how these rights can be exploited by the adversary to manipulate and gain influence in our lives.

## Legal Rights

### Unforgiveness

Unforgiveness is a common tactic the enemy employs to ensnare the people of God. Through scriptural legal rights, the adversary manipulates individuals, fostering unforgiveness. Unforgiveness is highly detrimental, fundamentally opposing the gospel and embracing an antichrist stance. If we were to summarize the gospel in a single word, it would be forgiveness. Forgiveness emerges as a mandate for believers—a non-negotiable obligation, commanded by God due to the forgiveness He has bestowed upon us.

*For if you forgive men for their sins, your heavenly Father will also forgive you. But if you do not forgive men for their sins, neither will your Father forgive your sins.*
Matthew 6:14-15

The severe consequences of unforgiveness often elude us; certain individuals are essentially condemning themselves to damnation over grudges. We assert that others "don't merit our forgiveness," yet the pivotal question arises: Do we merit the Father's forgiveness? Each of us has fallen short, with some committing grievous transgressions. Nonetheless, God embraces us, extending forgiveness through Christ. Despite identifying as believers and followers of the Way, we falter in practicing the very element that redeemed us. Though it may seem harsh, it stands justified.

The core essence of the cross embodies forgiveness, restoring us to God's initial and enduring purpose. Paul's directive in 1 Corinthians 11:1 urges us to emulate him as he emulates Christ. If we strive to mirror Christ, then embracing the primary essence of His earthly mission—forgiveness—should naturally follow.

Being "anti-Christ" signifies opposing or standing contrary to Christ, which is precisely the polar opposite stance.Opposing God's calling leads to yielding ground to the enemy. Unforgiveness cedes territory to the adversary, whereas alignment with God fosters His safeguard. Obedience to God situates us under heaven's authority, encompassing His rule, protection, and grace. However, adopting a contrary path places us outside heaven's jurisdiction, defying the kingdom's constitution that we should abide by. God highly regards His own Word even above His name (Psalms 138:2).

While unforgiveness may appear as a simple concept to overcome, and possibly the most fundamental for believers, it often remains a frequent issue among those we've prayed for during deliverance. Many individuals find that unforgiveness is a key factor holding them back and preventing them from breaking free of legal constraints. Addressing this foundational aspect of Christian faith is not only vital for deliverance but also for experiencing the true freedom found in Christ. Despite attempts to downplay unforgiveness as a common church topic, the reality is that many of us haven't truly confronted it within certain relationships or life experiences.

My encouragement to the leader is that you don't let Satan have a legal hold due to some grudge that might be lingering in your past. I tell my congregation all the time, "I won't go to hell for a grudge." Allow yourself to feel the freedom of forgiveness. The initial thought behind holding onto unforgiveness is that people don't deserve my forgiveness. But the truth is, we don't deserve Christ's forgiveness either, yet it was given to us anyway. By holding onto unforgiveness, we are going against the very message that saved us from sin and death. Let us be perpetuators of freedom and forgiveness so that we can best represent the gospel that was given on our behalf.

## Secrets/Lies

In many families and cultures, there are secrets hidden within their collective DNA. Proverbs 2:11 says, "Discretion will preserve you; understanding will keep you." However, when it comes to secrets, it's a different matter. Secrets create shadows within us, areas where we not only hide from others but often from God. When we keep secrets, these areas can become regions of captivity where the enemy gains a foothold. Discretion isn't just about guarding what God is doing in you, but also about being a confidant for others. What I've learned is that the difference between discretion and secrets is that secrets are burdens a person was never meant to carry alone; they weigh down areas meant for truth and transparency.

*Then Jesus said to those Jews who believed Him, "If you remain in My word, then you are truly My disciples. You shall know the truth, and the truth shall set you free*
John 8:31-32

Scripture emphasizes that the truth shall set you free. Though in context, it refers to the word of God and the teachings of Jesus, it's a fundamental principle that God always adheres to. When we explore the Scriptures, we find that Jesus frequently spoke about telling the truth, as seen in passages like John 8:45 and John 16:7. Most importantly, Jesus declared, "I am the way, the truth, and the life" (John 14:6). Jesus equated Himself with the concept of truth. This raises the question of how dangerous a lie or a secret, which essentially involves omitting the truth, can be. Consider this: a secret is a deliberate omission of the truth, and we often carry secrets out of love, to meet others' expectations, or due to the conditioning we've experienced. Keeping secrets can lock away areas that God intends to heal.

Let me provide you with a revised version: Consider this: The kingdom of heaven embodies a realm of transparency and illumination, while the kingdom of darkness signifies a domain of concealment and obscurity. The adversary often employs shadows to shroud himself, and in the context of communication, these shadows materialize as secrets and falsehoods. You might wonder why I associate lies with secrets. It's because lies contradict the truth and, in a sense, blaspheme against it when spoken. When we utter untruths, we deviate from God's counsel, truth, and principles.

*Therefore, putting away lying, let every man speak truthfully with his neighbor, for we are members of one another*
Ephesians 4:25

This scripture discusses the importance of speaking the truth to our neighbors. However, if we focus solely on the scripture, it emphasizes emulating Christ's actions towards our neighbors. This entails being genuinely truthful and communicating in truth as ambassadors of the kingdom. When we withhold the truth and utter lies, we commit blasphemy against the truth, preventing our freedom, as Scripture teaches that the truth will set us free.

## Soul Ties

A key question to better understand soul ties is, "To whom have I granted access?" Soul ties suggest that certain relationships can become overly entwined due to insufficient boundaries. These ties can form in various relationships, from friendships and family connections to intimate romantic relationships. An example of a positive soul tie or covenant relationship is seen in the bond between David and Jonathan. Like anything else, a beneficial concept can turn harmful when applied with the wrong boundaries or with the wrong person.

Jonathan and David serve as an excellent illustration of allowing the right person the appropriate access and maintaining suitable boundaries in the correct context. When comprehending soul ties, it's important to note that they are not inherently negative. It's our lack of maturity in relational intelligence or the actions and inability of others to love us properly that can adversely impact our relationships, leading us to grant access to the wrong individuals.

*When he had finished speaking to Saul, the soul of Jonathan was bound to the soul of David, so that Jonathan loved him as his own soul.*
1 Samuel 18:1

In this scripture, we encounter the precise wording of their souls being knit together, and due to the nature of their relationship, it was a healthy bond. You might wonder why, then, soul ties are associated with granting a legal right or legal access to the enemy. This is because there is potential for granting the wrong kind of access to the wrong types of individuals.

*"When Shechem, the son of Hamor the Hivite, prince of the land, saw her, he took her and lay with her and defiled her. He was very smitten by Dinah the daughter of Jacob, and he loved the girl and spoke kindly to her."*
Genesis 34:2-3

Shechem faced consequences because a connection was established through coerced sexual acts, leading to the formation of soul ties. Both sexual and emotional bonds that intertwine individuals were at play in this case. He was deeply affected and insisted that his father arrange a marriage with the girl. Many times, we engage in improper interactions, whether it's premarital sex, sex without the intent of marriage, or emotional relationships lacking boundaries, which leave us vulnerable and accessible to soul ties. These soul ties grant access not only to people but also to the spiritual elements within and from them.

When I guide people through deliverance, I frequently inquire about the patterns they're encountering. In many cases, they mention experiencing sudden feelings of depression, anxiety, or anger, which they've never felt before. Often, during counseling, the emergence of a person, whether in the form of an emotional or intimate relationship, becomes apparent. When I ask these individuals whether that person deals with depression, anxiety, or anger, the answer is often, "Absolutely, yes."

We may encounter soul ties within our families due to involvement in witchcraft, where curses or spirits gain access through the bloodline or create soul ties with a specific family member. While the intentions of these relationships may be well-meaning, a lack of spiritual protection or boundaries can lead to exposure to the same occultism that affects the family or that particular member.

For example, if a family member with whom you have a soul tie has made an agreement with a witch or warlock, the actions of that family member, along with the legal right granted by witchcraft, may allow demons to enter both the family member and you due to the connection. While these are issues in the context of deliverance, the solution often involves not only spiritual protection through prayer but also the practical step of setting appropriate boundaries. This allows for maintaining a healthy relationship with those individuals without granting them complete access.

## Demonic Agreements & Occultism

What are you in agreement with? The truth is that we often form agreements with specific people or things, and these agreements can take the form of aligning with certain principles or ideologies that people hold or simply becoming actively involved in something. As the Bible says, "faith without works is dead," so adding works to what we believe and agree to can lead to destruction when done in the wrong direction. Regardless of how these agreements manifest, it's clear that agreement is a powerful principle in the Word. However, agreement does not always guarantee positive access.

We've previously discussed the consequences of forming strong connections or soul ties, and a similar dynamic occurs when we enter into agreements with certain ideas or places. For instance, if you commit your life to Christ, you become aligned and connected to Christ, which can have positive spiritual implications. Jesus said, "My yoke is easy" (Matthew 11:30), implying that in life, you are either yoked to Him or something else, and life consists of what we agree to be in agreement with. Conversely, aligning with the wrong ideologies or the wrong people in our lives can lead to negative consequences.

You might wonder how this relates to demonic agreements. The
truth is that demonic agreements can take various forms, from chants and rituals to seemingly simple alignments with things that are not in line with Christ's nature and His Word. Thus, if you agree with the Doctrine of Devils, as mentioned in 1 Timothy 4:1, which warns us not to, it can open us up to anti-Christ spirits, such as the spirit of religion, for example.

Another type of agreement is with secret organizations and fraternities/sororities. These agreements can inadvertently open doors to negative spiritual influences. Personally, I've experienced the breaking of a generational curse related to Freemasonry, which resulted from my ancestors aligning with something contrary to God's will (idolatry), allowing demonic influences to pass through the bloodline. Similarly, we've also broken curses and demonic influences from people who aligned with other secret societies, such as specific fraternities and sororities, which had unintended spiritual consequences.

*Peter said to her, "How is it that you have agreed together to test the Spirit of the Lord? Look! The feet of those who have buried your husband are at the door, and they will carry you out"*
Acts 5:9

In this verse, we observe an unholy agreement between a couple who rejected the Spirit of God and committed blasphemy against the Holy Spirit, resulting in severe consequences, including death for both of them. It's important to emphasize that we can't dismiss this as an Old Testament occurrence because it took place in the New Testament, within the early church. This act can be understood as an anti-Christ agreement that directly contradicted God's will, thus constituting blasphemy against the Holy Spirit. This example illustrates how we can inadvertently form agreements, even with those we love, based on misguided principles and foundations.

An agreement between two parties holds power in both the spiritual and physical realms. In business, people shake hands to signify an agreement, symbolizing a firm and aligned relationship. Depending on which state you live in, laws may even uphold a verbal agreement without a written contract. Companies can be bought out, merged, or change trajectory through agreements. In the spiritual realm, agreement is just as powerful, both in positive and negative ways.

*Again I say to you, that if two of you agree on earth about anything they ask, it will be done for them by My Father who is in heaven*
Matthew 18:19

When Jesus spoke about the power of agreement, He highlighted the significance of people coming together to accomplish God's work and make requests of their Heavenly Father. The power of agreement is a fundamental principle within the kingdom. However, just as the enemy often distorts and misuses kingdom principles to gain legal rights, it's essential to remember that the Word of God serves as the kingdom's constitution, endowing its words with great power.

So, when the enemy exploits the power of agreement to

manipulate and bind an individual or a group, ultimately hindering their efforts, we can discern how the adversary sets people up for failure. One example is the enemy telling you lies about yourself to get you to agree with them, such as 'I'm stupid,' 'I'm lazy,' 'I'm broke,' 'I'm not smart enough,' 'I'm not pretty enough,' or 'I'm not strong enough.' These are all lies the enemy uses to convince us that we are thinking these things, and ultimately, to get us to speak them, as life and death are in the power of the tongue, as shown in Proverbs 18:21.

*There must not be found among you anyone who makes his son or his daughter pass through the fire, or who uses divination, or uses witchcraft, or an interpreter of omens, or a sorcerer, or one who casts spells, or a spiritualist, or an occultist, or a necromancer. For all that do these things are an abomination to the Lord, and because of these abominations the Lord your God will drive them out from before you. You must be blameless before the Lord your God*
Deuteronomy 18:10-13

As believers, we understand that the enemy will gain access any way he can. Witchcraft practices often involve giving and receiving gifts, such as items, food, or money, to bring about agreement. My wife and I have seen instances where people have poured into our ministry, only for my wife to become stricken with an ailment. Through prayer, it was revealed to us that a monetary gift was given with the wrong spirit (demonic), and we needed to break off the demonic agreement that came with the funds. We have since adopted the practice of automatically praying to break off demonic covenants and agreements when we receive offerings to our ministry. Whether or not the individual had true intentions, we may sometimes be demonically influenced, and this is where discernment is essential for the saints of Jesus.

God has consistently opposed activities and entities that go against His Word. Any powers, agreements, or groups aligning themselves with an anti-Christ spirit should be avoided. While agreements may grant legal authority, it's important to note that witchcraft and cult-like practices derive their power from illegal access. Our access to spiritual power comes as children of the Most High, through our position as sons and daughters by inheritance.

# 3

# A Spiritual War

Perhaps one of the most intriguing and under-discussed revelations in church circles is the acknowledgment that we are actively engaged in a spiritual battle. Through rebirth in faith, we gain access to the spiritual realm, becoming heirs as beloved sons and daughters of the Most High. In this new identity, we are transformed into spiritual warriors, ambassadors with the authority to mediate, and members of a royal priesthood. We are not only seated in high places; we are also commissioned as ambassadors, ready to fulfill our divine roles.

One of the enemy's most significant accomplishments is diverting the people of God into conflicts with mere human concerns and distracting us with the things right in front of us. We often find ourselves engrossed in activities like binge-watching Netflix, neglecting the vital practice of fervent and consistent prayer. Many of us attend church services that lack genuine spiritual power, relying on recycled information while failing to manifest the true power that the Church is meant to exhibit.

It's crucial to recognize that the early church in Acts, often held up as a model in contemporary evangelicalism, operated with a greater abundance of power, revelation, and unity than we see today. To truly flourish as a church, we must establish ourselves firmly on the foundation of Jesus Christ, the cornerstone, and allow the Holy Spirit to be our guiding force.

There is an increasingly urgent need for Apostolic Reform within the church. This reform is essential to revive a powerful and revelatory movement that can effectively challenge the forces and authorities that have obstructed the progress of God's people for far too long.

> *"For our fight is not against flesh and blood, but against principalities, against powers, against the rulers of the darkness of this world, and against spiritual forces of evil in the heavenly places."*
> Ephesians 6:12

The church has been blinded by focusing on individuals rather than recognizing the forces at work behind the scenes. There are demonic powers pulling the strings, affecting the world and its people. Scripture emphasizes that our battle is not against flesh and blood but against principalities, powers, rulers of darkness, and spiritual forces of evil. This reveals that we are engaged in a spiritual war, not just against a government of darkness, but a militant force opposing the body of Christ. The kingdom of darkness operates in shadows and secrets, with evil agendas. As the body of Christ, we must not only be aware of this spiritual war but also arm ourselves and boldly fulfill our purpose. We should avoid the distractions of fleshly conflicts and instead operate in the realm where God has given us the power to bind and loose.

*Jesus answered him, "Blessed are you, Simon son of Jonah, for flesh and blood has not revealed this to you, but My Father who is in heaven. And I tell you that you are Peter, and on this rock I will build My church, and the gates of Hades shall not prevail against it. I will give you the keys of the kingdom of heaven, and whatever you bind on earth shall be bound in heaven, and whatever you loose on earth shall be loosed in heaven."*
Matthew 16:17-19

Here, we not only witness God's promise that hell won't prevail against the church, and that the forces of darkness will be underfoot, but it also speaks to the governmental power bestowed upon Peter and the church in the spiritual realm. There is spiritual authority ingrained in our DNA as believers. Mark 16:17-18 assures believers of the power to cast out demons and heal the sick – a supernatural authority inherent in our identity. However, it also signifies that this power is given for a purpose: to actively combat the kingdom of darkness and dismantle the works of the enemy.

The Matthew 16: 17-19 passage also mentions the keys of the Kingdom given to Peter and the church. Entrusting keys signifies trust from the Father, granting us spiritual authority and access not only to power but to a higher level of anointing in His kingdom. Consider this: would you give your house keys to someone you did not trust? God is granting us access not only to levels of power and authority but to His kingdom. This gift of trust significantly empowers believers. Unfortunately, we often settle for less, not only failing to wield this power against the kingdom of darkness but also lacking belief in it. Religion has influenced the church in a way that leads us to explain away the authority given to us.

When we explain away the authority given to us, rather than embracing the anointing of authority bestowed upon us, we disarm ourselves at our very core. It's akin to relinquishing a spiritual inheritance, distancing ourselves from our equipped potential. Allowing religion to bind us, we shift away from the promise given to the church that the gates of Hades will not prevail against us.

## Given Authority in the Battlefield and the Courts of Heaven

As believers and individuals called to engage in spiritual warfare, we are not merely warriors on the battlefield but also participants in the heavenly courts. Through our inheritance in Christ, we have access to and authority in the Courts of Heaven. God hasn't called us solely to fight as ground-level soldiers; He is also bestowing judicial power upon believers

## Soldiers

We find ourselves in an ongoing battle between light and darkness. Despite operating from a position of victory (to be discussed in more detail later), we must continue to actively participate in the spiritual warfare assigned to us as the hands and feet of Jesus Christ. As agents tasked with this responsibility, it is our duty to combat the forces of darkness and dismantle demonic principles attempting to manifest on Earth.

*"Endure hard times as a good soldier of Jesus Christ. No soldier on active duty entangles himself with civilian affairs, that he may please the enlisting officer."*
2 Timothy 2:3-4

The scripture instructs us to endure difficult times as good soldiers of Jesus Christ. This not only outlines the expectations Christ has for His soldiers but also explicitly identifies us as soldiers of Christ. The passage further emphasizes that an active-duty soldier avoids entanglement in civilian affairs to please the enlisting officer. In our case, Jesus Christ is our enlisting officer who has called and sent us. Getting caught up in civilian affairs distracts us from the responsibilities of a soldier – fighting necessary battles, occupying designated territories, and fulfilling the missions assigned by God.

*"Proclaim this among the nations: Consecrate a war! Stir up the mighty men! Let all the men of war draw near and rise."*
Joel 3:9

We need to stir up the mighty men and women of God; we need all men and women of war to draw near and rise. When we grasp that we are inherently wired for battle from birth, we recognize the inherent power bestowed upon us. As believers, we are soldiers summoned to the battlefield, engaging in a fight of which, whether acknowledged or not, we have long been casualties. Some may question the need to be a soldier, and my response would be that I prefer being a soldier rather than becoming a casualty or collateral damage. Instead of succumbing to the warfare waged against the people of God in this world, we have been given the opportunity to harness the God-given power within us and become a formidable force for the Kingdom of Light.

Jesus Christ, the commanding officer of believers, intercedes for individuals like you, the reader of this book, to step into your God-ordained purpose as a soldier for the Kingdom. Our calling is as diverse as those enlisted by Christ to participate in both battlefield warfare and the courts. As soldiers, we also serve as judicial representatives.

## Judicial Enforcer

Although there is not a specific technical term for our role as believers with access to the courts, for the sake of this book, I have chosen to label our role as "Judicial Enforcers." Frequently, we recognize God as the Creator, Savior, Redeemer, and Healer, yet we may overlook His role as Judge.

*"But you have come to Mount Zion and to the city of the living God, the heavenly Jerusalem, and to an innumerable company of angels; to the general assembly and church of the firstborn, who are enrolled in heaven; to God, the Judge of all; and to the spirits of the righteous ones made perfect."*
Hebrews 12:22-23

The scripture refers to God as the Judge of all. Recognizing God's role as Judge in the Heavenly Courts helps us understand how we should interact with Him. Just as you wouldn't approach a Judge without honor, proper reverence, or respect for their title and office, we similarly need to approach God in a manner that acknowledges His authority and position.

In your role as a Judicial Enforcer, you function as a Defense Attorney for the broken seeking healing and deliverance, a Prosecuting Attorney against the kingdom of darkness, and a Courtroom Witness to the supernatural realm of the Courts of Heaven.

*Defense Attorney*

When we act as Defense Attorneys within the Courts of Heaven, we see our involvement in this mission coming to fruition as vessels of healing and deliverance. When we intercede and facilitate deliverance for others, we partake in accessing the Heavenly Courts through prayer. This endeavor contributes to liberating individuals from demonic influence, breaking generational curses, and dismantling the works of witchcraft.

*If I have the gift of prophecy, and understand all mysteries and all knowledge, and if I have all faith, so that I could remove mountains, and have not love, I am nothing.*
1 Corinthians 13:2

A Defense Attorney is responsible for legally representing someone charged with a crime. Similarly, a deliverance minister, when operating in the spiritual realm, assumes a comparable role. This role involves breaking generational curses by guiding individuals through repentant prayers for their family and identifying the origins of curses affecting their bloodline. It may also include casting out demons, dismantling their longstanding influence on an individual, or breaking the grip of witchcraft that affects them emotionally, financially, or spiritually. When standing in the gap for someone and accessing the Courts of Heaven, you function as their Defense Attorney. In the realm of deliverance, our purpose is to extend love and aid in their healing journey. It's crucial to understand that the ministry of deliverance is not one of judgement or aggression but, rather, of love and compassion. Simply put, without love, one cannot serve as a vessel of deliverance.

*Put Me in remembrance; let us plead together; state your cause, that you may be justified.*
Isaiah 43:26

The New King James Version replaces the word "justified" with "acquitted," clearly incorporating legal terminology. Additionally, it changes "cause" to "case," instructing us to "state your case." When we examine these legal terms and recognize that "cause" and "justified" in the context of this passage refer to courtroom language, we discern the importance of addressing this matter. This verse in Isaiah provides a precise directive from the Lord. When we comprehend that we can engage in the same process for ourselves and others—presenting our case before the court and aiding others through it—we gain insight into an elevated level of authority. It unveils a dimension of our role as sons and daughters that we might not have fully explored before.

## *Prosecuting Attorney*

In addition to serving as Defense Attorneys for those we are called to minister to, we also function as prosecuting attorneys against the kingdom of darkness. As Judicial Enforcers, we fulfill God's mandate by exposing darkness, condemning evil, and annihilating the works of Satan.

*"And do not have fellowship with the unfruitful works of darkness; instead, expose them."*
Ephesians 5:11

Here, we encounter two directives: a call to the way we live, urging us not to align with darkness, and a mandate to expose it. The first concept, avoiding fellowship with darkness, involves aligning our principles, values, and conduct with the light of God. People perceive our associations by observing our actions and words. Participating in unfruitful works of darkness can lead others to see us as participants in that darkness. This underscores the importance of consecrating our entire lives, continually striving for greater alignment with God at every stage of our spiritual growth. This includes our speech, conduct, the media and entertainment we engage with, and even the depth of fellowship we maintain with others. When we focus on the right things, centered on Jesus and guided by the Spirit, we can embody the truths that act as a light to the world, illuminating the lives of those around us. It is crucial to allow our lives, and the way we lead them, to serve as a beacon for those who observe and are influenced by our journey. The role of exposing darkness originates from the light that emanates from believers as they live set-apart lives.

*The light of the body is the eye. Therefore, if your eye is clear, your whole body will be full of light. But if your eye is unclear, your whole body will be full of darkness. Therefore, if the light that is in you is darkness, how great is that darkness!*
*Matthew 6:22-23*

It is stated that the eye is the light of the body, and if the eye is clear, the whole body is full of light. When we direct our gaze toward the right things—fixing our eyes on the correct focal points and avoiding the entanglements of desires or demonic distractions—we can experience the full light intended for believers. Consequently, we become like lighthouses wherever we are, a consistent source of light and illumination that exposes darkness. It's important to acknowledge that this isn't always an easy path. Understanding that light reveals darkness means it may impact those around us. Sometimes, our mere presence can illuminate aspects of others' lives they wish to change or feel insecure about. Recognize that any anger manifested may not be directed at you but rather at what you, and the light you bring, have exposed. The same principle applies when it comes to shedding light on cultural darkness and contributing to the world's education in the principles of the Kingdom of Heaven.

One responsibility of a Prosecuting Attorney is to construct a case and counter the arguments presented by the opposing counsel. Remember, Ephesians 6:12 emphasizes that our struggle is "against principalities, against powers, against the rulers of the darkness of this world, and against spiritual forces of evil in heavenly places." As Prosecuting Attorneys, it is our duty to enter the Courts of Heaven and engage in spiritual warfare, when we conduct cease and desists against the enemy by binding every demonic and dark influence attempting to take root in our sphere. Simultaneously, we loose the things of Heaven in every place we are called to occupy.

In fulfilling these dual roles, standing in the gap entails not only combating darkness as a Prosecuting Attorney against the forces of evil but also defending and interceding for those who are afflicted, in pain, and suffering, acting as a Defense Attorney. Additionally, we assume the role of a heavenly witness in the Courts of Heaven, capable of observing judicial movements in the spiritual realm.

## Court Room Witness

Comprehending our role as witnesses extends beyond the conventional understanding of the word. We are not merely individuals who provide an account of spiritual occurrences; we also serve as witnesses to the power of the courts and act as ambassadors for the Judge Himself.

> *"Then he showed me Joshua, the high priest, standing before the angel of the Lord, and Satan standing at his right hand to accuse him. And the Lord said to Satan, 'The Lord rebuke you, Satan! The Lord who has chosen Jerusalem rebukes you! Is this not a burning brand taken out of the fire?' Now Joshua had on filthy garments and was standing before the angel. And he said to those standing*

*before him, 'Take off his filthy garments.' Then he said, 'See that I have removed from you your iniquity, and I will clothe you with rich robes.' And I said, 'Let them place a pure turban on his head.' So they put a pure turban on his head and garments on him. And the angel of the Lord was standing by. And the angel of the Lord admonished Joshua, saying, 'Thus says the Lord of Hosts: If you walk in My ways and keep My charge, then you will judge My house and guard My courts, and I will give you access to these who are standing here.'"*
Zechariah 3:1-7

Zechariah is literally brought into the heavens in the spirit realm to witness court proceedings. Joshua, the high priest (not the same Joshua who was Moses' predecessor), undergoes a form of deliverance in the heavenly courts. Both Joshua and Zechariah are brought into another realm—specifically, the courts of heaven. One of the mistakes made by the body of Christ is neglecting the gift of being a seer or prophet who can traverse different realms. The reason some people fail to experience miracles and grasp the full power of our inheritance as believers is that they settle for a limited, nonspiritual, and religious perspective of who God is and what He calls the church to be.

As believers, we must be prepared for everything God wants to do and reveal to us. While prophets like Zechariah are brought into other realms by God, it's crucial to recognize that all experiences in the spirit realm that are of God occur through the Holy Spirit. For example, one cannot practice witchcraft like astral projection and claim that God led them there. When the Holy Spirit intends to transport you spiritually,

He will do so. It's not something to strive for independently. Unfortunately, some individuals engage in illicit spiritual activities, transitioning from a genuine interest in the supernatural aspects of God's power to pursuing it through anti-Christ and spiritually unlawful means.

In this grand spiritual battle, let us understand that we are not mere bystanders but mighty warriors, intricately designed for victory. Our purpose is to obliterate the works of darkness, establish dominion, and occupy for the kingdom of God. Embrace your role with the assurance that you are wired for victory!

# 4

# Armed & Dangerous

As believers, never perceive yourself as defenseless; recognize that you are armed and dangerous from the moment you inherit salvation. You possess weapons that are inaccessible to the enemy and the world. Above all, you wield a sword capable of cutting down any adversary and conquering every spiritual attack—a weapon God values as equal of His own name.

## Use The Word as a Weapon!

*"Take the helmet of salvation and the sword of the Spirit, which is the word of God."*
Ephesians 6:17

Understanding that the Word of God is not merely a source of information and transformation from within, but also a powerful weapon against the kingdom of darkness, is crucial. It has the capacity to dismantle any enemy and foil any plot.

Recognizing the symbolism of swords is significant as well—they were a prevalent weapon in biblical times, representing not only defense but also offense in the midst of battle.

While a helmet, symbolizing our salvation through Christ, provides protection, the sword is not just a defensive tool; it is a weapon against all the forces of hell and anything that opposes you and the Church. The authority of Scripture alone surpasses every demon, curse on your bloodline, and any attempt of witchcraft or spell trying to take root.

*"I will worship toward Your holy temple, and praise Your name for Your lovingkindness and for Your truth; for You have exalted Your word above all Your name."*
Psalms 138:2

God elevates His Word even above His own name; its authority resonates uniquely in the spiritual realm. Consider that our salvation comes through Christ, referred to as the Word made flesh in the Bible (John 1:14). Grasp the profound power of His Word—not merely the utterances from the Father's lips or the Scriptures we believe in, but Christ Himself, seated on the heavenly throne at the right hand of the Father. Through salvation, we gain access to the formidable weapon that is God's Word.

When we wield God's Word as a weapon, it's essential to recognize that it not only affects what we direct it towards but also impacts ourselves. It is a double-edged sword, a precise and penetrating tool sharper than any other weapon. The Word should consistently have an internal impact on us, ensuring that we can authentically live out the Scriptures we wield against the kingdom of darkness, embodying our role as Soldiers and Judicial Enforcers for the Kingdom of Heaven. Remember that God instructed the prophet to consume the scroll first (Ezekiel 3:1); the word of God is not just a weapon but also a catalyst for change within us. We are meant to be transformed by the Word before effectively using it.

*"For the word of God is alive and active, sharper than any two-edged sword, piercing even to the division of soul and spirit, of joints and marrow, and able to judge the thoughts and intents of the heart."*
Hebrews 4:12

The passage begins by stating that the Word of God is alive and active. When we grasp this, we understand why individuals can read the same passage throughout their lives and gain new insights each time. It's not merely a book of information; it is the spoken Word of the Lord. Consider that His voice spoke the universe into existence, and His Word, held above His own name, is not only powerful but alive and active, continually moving on the earth. Described as sharper than any two-edged sword, I received a revelation years ago that it's called a two-edged sword because it impacts us personally as much as we use it against the kingdom of darkness or to help others. There's always a personal impact to His Word. When the scripture states that it pierces even to the division of soul and spirit, we witness this during deliverance sessions. As we speak the Word of the Lord, demons wail and are cast out by the scripture itself. Above all, the passage illustrates that scripture can help us judge, alongside our discernment, the motives of people's hearts and thoughts. This discernment is crucial in spiritual warfare, aiding us in understanding with whom to align.

## Our Weapons Are Not Carnal

As warriors in the Kingdom of Heaven, our weapons are not like those of ordinary soldiers in battle. These weapons are meant for pulling down strongholds, casting down imaginations, and dismantling everything that exalts itself against the knowledge of God.

*"For though we walk in the flesh, we do not war according to the flesh. For the weapons of our warfare are not carnal, but mighty through God to the pulling down of strongholds, casting down imaginations and every high thing that exalts itself against the knowledge of God, bringing every thought into captivity to the obedience of Christ, and being ready to punish all disobedience when your obedience is complete."*
2 Corinthians 10:3-6

This passage emphasizes that even though we live in the physical realm, our battles are not fought on a physical level. It highlights that our true identity is not confined to the material aspects of life but is rooted in spiritual realities, constituting our inheritance. The warfare we engage in is spiritual, guided by the Holy Spirit. The weapons at our disposal are not worldly or fleshly; instead, they derive their might from God and have a spiritual origin and efficacy. These powerful tools can be employed to dismantle strongholds, challenge imaginations, and overcome anything that opposes the knowledge of God.

The passage underscores the effectiveness of these spiritual weapons in various forms of spiritual warfare.

By grasping the truths of the Spirit realm and supernatural warfare, we gain the ability to confront the adversary on the true battleground. It's crucial to recognize that our struggle is not against mere flesh and blood. Often, when we are not guided by the Holy Spirit there's a tendency to misinterpret both the battlefield and the arsenal available to us in combating the enemy. This misunderstanding can leave us vulnerable, distracted, and deceived, ultimately causing us to miss out on our rightful inheritance of victory.

## Types of Weapons

Recognizing the arsenal or variety of weapons available to us holds significant importance. I could dedicate an entire book solely to this subject, and although I cannot detail every single weapon or strategy in this chapter, that might be a project for another time. For now, I wish to compile a list of some frequently underestimated spiritual weapons and emphasize the depth of power they possess.

We've previously discussed God's Word and its nature as the sword of the Spirit, capable of cutting down and destroying all works of darkness. However, believers—those who identify as Sons and Daughters in the Kingdom—have access to numerous other weapons. Let's delve into what is within our armory.

# Prayer

Prayer constitutes a foundational and indispensable aspect of the believer's relationship with God, facilitating access to the inheritance bestowed upon them as sons and daughters of Christ. Prayer is a designated meeting ground between humanity and the Lord—a point of communication graciously open to us through His love. Prevalent misconceptions about prayer, stemming from oversimplified messages and dry theology, may suggest a lack of power in prayer. However, its significance surpasses mere dialogue and communication; it is pivotal for fostering relationships and encompasses a profound spiritual dimension. Jesus Christ, as our exemplar, manifested a lifestyle characterized by continuous communion with the Father. As the Chief Apostle, it falls upon God's Apostolic Church to emulate this example, integrating fervent prayer into our own lives.

Have we ever pondered the abundance of miraculous prayer testimonies in the past, or the prevalence of miracles in churches from other regions, contrasting with the apparent limitation of miraculous power in Western church culture? Numerous ministries witness revival, where healing and casting out demons are regular occurrences. However, if we're honest with ourselves, the mainstream church—even those more recognized—often lacks the level of faith needed to embrace such experiences. Even if this faith exists within individuals, it might not be ingrained in the culture of the churches we are establishing. Now is the time to alter that fundamental DNA and usher in a transformative shift.

*"Pray without ceasing."*
1 Thessalonians 5:17

Though this may be the shortest passage I will quote in this book, it might be one of the most needed and relevant scriptures in the whole book. One of the things I have had to learn during this Apostolic journey is that prayer must be continuous. When the Lord says in Scripture to pray without ceasing, this declaration is such a vital part of the believer's walk. Remember, the enemy and the warfare that will come to your doorstep will not wait for the right timing or when it is practical within your schedule to put up a fight and begin to war. This is why praying without ceasing is so needed and necessary, so we can truly be ready in season and out (2 Timothy 4:2).

*"Confess your faults to one another and pray for one another, that you may be healed. The effective, fervent prayer of a righteous man accomplishes much."*
James 5:16

When dissecting this passage, there is an emphasis on positioning ourselves as intercessors. It begins by urging confession of sins to one another and underscores that the prayers of a righteous individual have great efficacy. While it is true that we attain righteousness through Christ, believers are held to a standard by God. Though God is faithful to forgive our sins, we shouldn't misuse His grace as a crutch and fail to pursue righteousness.

As we earnestly move toward righteousness, God responds with His blessing for obedience. These blessings, in turn, enhance the effectiveness of our prayers, drawing favor. Hence, one crucial aspect of arming ourselves in prayer is to live according to the standard of righteousness prescribed by God. This not only sharpens our prayer weapon against the kingdom of darkness but also makes it potent for advancing the Kingdom of Heaven.

This point is further underscored by the passage's opening, which declares the importance of confessing our sins to one another. Following this confession, the passage asserts that healing will ensue. Bringing our areas of sin and disobedience before the throne of God, seeking His forgiveness while humbly confessing to one another, invokes grace for healing. When we position ourselves as vessels worthy of God's ear and anointing for healing and breakthrough, we undergo a sharpening process, transforming into the secret weapon that God has always intended us to be against the forces of evil.

> "Is anyone among you suffering? Let him pray. Is anyone merry? Let him sing psalms."
> James 5:13

In the midst of war, you contend with various challenges—not just the immediate warfare but everything else in your life simultaneously. It's crucial to grasp that prayer extends beyond spiritual warfare, healing, and deliverance; it encompasses all aspects, including any form of suffering. Clearly stated, if anyone is experiencing suffering, the directive is explicit: let them pray. Prayer serves as the gateway for breakthroughs, acting as the catalyst for the Breaker's anointing. This anointing has the power not only to liberate those for whom you intercede but also to alleviate any suffering in your own life.

# Fasting

In my experience as a pastor and senior leader, one weapon I've observed missing from many people's arsenal is fasting. Unfortunately, fasting is often seen as optional or even deemed religious and unnecessary. However, the reality couldn't be further from the truth, particularly when it comes to the realm of spiritual warfare.

*"But this kind does not go out except by prayer and fasting."*
Matthew 17:21

I must highlight one of the most concerning aspects of certain Bible translations regarding this verse. Some versions have entirely omitted the part stating that certain demons can only be cast out through prayer and fasting. Whether influenced by religious biases or a demonic agenda, this omission suggests an effort to keep believers unaware that prayer and fasting constitute a secret weapon against the forces of darkness, including demons, witchcraft, and spiritual hindrances. While we've discussed prayer previously, fasting serves as a catalyst for whatever you bring before heaven, making it an essential component in the spiritual strategy of warfare.

Any minister of deliverance or believer with experience in casting out demons can affirm that fasting enhances breakthrough—not just for the one receiving deliverance but also for the vessel facilitating it. Fasting serves as an accelerant to the anointing during prayer and open enough for the Holy

Spirit's will to be done more during the deliverance session, allowing individuals to experience a deeper level of cleansing during a deliverance session.

*"Is this not the fast that I have chosen: to loose the bonds of wickedness, to undo the heavy burdens, to let the oppressed go free, and to break every yoke?"*
Isaiah 58:6

This scripture explicitly portrays the chosen fast as a means of deliverance and breakthrough. Recognizing the impact of fasting on breakthroughs can unveil new dimensions in the supernatural realm within your faith journey. It illustrates fasting as a method to release individuals from heavy burdens, liberate the oppressed, and break every yoke.

*"As they worshipped the Lord and fasted, the Holy Spirit said, 'Set apart for Me Barnabas and Saul for the work to which I have called them.'"*
Acts 13:2

It's noteworthy to mention that a significant breakthrough attainable through fasting is not only hearing from the Lord but also finding direction. This holds true in the context of seeking a strategy in spiritual warfare. Just as the Holy Spirit communicated with believers who were gathered, worshiping, and fasting together, we can similarly expect the Holy Spirit to guide us in matters related to spiritual warfare.

# Prophecy

Prophecy, considered a weapon, may seem unfamiliar to some. However, it goes beyond merely foretelling future events or gaining insights into Kairos moments. It involves words of knowledge regarding people's past or future and what lies ahead for them. Prophecy can genuinely function as a weapon in deliverance. During deliverance sessions, prophesying about someone's purpose and divine plans for them often leads to the manifestation of demons. These entities fear the person's prophetic destiny and aim to disrupt their heavenly calling with chaos. It's essential to realize that prophecy involves not only conveying heavenly decrees but also revealing the heart and mind of the Lord. The things of the Kingdom of Light perpetually expose the workings of the kingdom of darkness.

*"I fell at his feet to worship him. But he said to me, 'See that you do not do that. I am your fellow servant, and of your brothers who hold the testimony of Jesus. Worship God! For the testimony of Jesus is the spirit of prophecy.'"*
Revelation 19:10

*"They overcame him by the blood of the Lamb and by the word of their testimony, and they loved not their lives unto death."*
Revelation 12:11

In these two passages, we not only discover that the testimony of Jesus is the spirit of prophecy, but we also recognize its prophetic connection to overcoming through the blood of the Lamb, or the blood of Jesus, and the word of our testimony.

Prophesying someone's God-ordained destiny in the name of Jesus utilizes prophecy to declare the testimony that will conquer those opposing forces. Through prophecy, you are foretelling the outcome of their breakthrough and predicting the result of that season of growth. This act unsettles demons, as it solidifies the impending breakthrough that will dismantle the bondage keeping them anchored and stagnant. Therefore, when we encounter a standstill in deliverance sessions, it's crucial to allow the Lord to speak to us about that person's destiny. Begin to prophesy over that individual, declaring the things that the Lord has already foretold for them. Empower them with the advance revelation of their testimony through the spirit of prophecy, which is indeed the testimony of Jesus.

Prophetic insight not only grants us the ability to perceive Kairos moments in prophetic timing but also provides a profound understanding of the supernatural. Prophets and those with prophetic gifting function as both supernatural warriors and spiritual scouts. Venturing into other dimensions within the Spiritual Realm, individuals with prophetic gifts gain access to intelligence that is uniquely derived from their abilities to see and hear in the Spiritual Realm. God utilizes Seers to assist the church in developing a battle strategy, much like generals rely on scouts to gather intelligence for strategic planning.

*"Then the king of Aram was fighting against Israel, and he took counsel with his servants, saying, 'At such and such a place will be my camp.' But the man of God sent word to the king of Israel, saying, 'Take care not to pass through this place, for the Arameans are marching down there.' The king of Israel sent word to the place*

*of which the man of God spoke. He warned him and was on his guard there more than once."*
2 Kings 6:8-10

The prophet Elisha employed prophetic insight to advise the king on battle strategy, creating confusion in the enemy's camp. Recognizing that accessing and utilizing the prophetic for strategy and warfare allows us to stay ahead of the enemy's plans. Being a prophetic strategist positions the Kingdom of Light in a realm of strategic excellence when engaging in warfare. It's imperative to comprehend the potency of prophecy as a weapon against the kingdom of darkness, serving as a source of fire, power, and intelligence gathering.

## Calling in Reinforcements

We were never meant to face battles alone! The intention was never for us to navigate life, tackle challenges, or overcome obstacles in isolation. Truthfully, the reason we often find ourselves stuck while overcoming certain obstacles is that we attempt to rely solely on our own strength. While we have God, He also provides relationships that, when nurtured in a healthy way, can love, heal, and protect us.

It's crucial to remember that God didn't assign you a solo mission; instead, He sent you on a mission that requires a team with reinforcements. Every aspect of your life is intended to be approached in unity and fellowship with others. With a few exceptions for personal matters, our lives are meant to be surrounded by those who can come alongside us with love and unity. Unfortunately, due to people's wounds in relationships or their struggle to cultivate real intimacy, there can be an unhealthy self-dependency that contradicts the way God designed us to live. Jesus Himself didn't embark on a solo mission; He enlisted a group of people with whom He had relationships to work alongside. Besides His 12 disciples, He also collaborated with others during various phases of His earthly walk.

*"For just as we have many parts in one body, and not all parts have the same function, so we, being many, are one body in Christ, and all are parts of one another."*
Romans 12:4-5

This passage provides profound insights into understanding the body of Christ, much like how our physical body functions in harmony. Every part working together is how the body of Christ is meant to operate. Unfortunately, we have divided ourselves through divisive behaviors. Recognizing the importance of relationships can lead us to a more effective way of being connected and moving together. If we can appreciate each other's unique gifts and differences, we can utilize them collectively rather than fostering envy or neglecting the strengths found in people's differences. Consider it this way: if we acknowledge that each part of the body, or our brothers and sisters in Christ, operates with distinct gifts and areas of operation, we gain access to a more potent offensive front in warfare.

*"Two are better than one, because there is a good reward for their*

*labor together. For if they fall, one will help up his companion. But woe to him who is alone when he falls and has no one to help him up. Also, if two lie down together, they will keep warm; but how can one keep warm by himself? And if someone might overpower another by himself, two together can withstand him. A threefold cord is not quickly broken."*
Ecclesiastes 4:9-12

The passage emphasizes that two are better than one and that there is a great reward for their joint labor. Regardless of our individual efforts, working together with fellow members of the body of Christ yields greater rewards. A crucial aspect highlighted in the text is that if one falls, the other can help them up. When we isolate ourselves, attempting to be solo heroes, we risk falling without someone to assist us in getting back up. Companionship is essential; David had Jonathan, Elijah had Elisha, and Jesus and the disciples had each other, and the list continues. So, when discussing warfare, it's crucial to understand that it was never meant to be a solo endeavor. Instead, it was designed as a collective campaign with brothers and sisters in arms and reinforcements at the ready.

Matthew 28:16-20 paints a picture of the Great Commission, where Jesus sends us into the world to make disciples of all nations. It's important to note that He called them to do this as a collective group, issuing marching orders to the generals of His army to be sent out and effectively serve the Kingdom. Our purpose is to raise up an army that doesn't just follow us but, more importantly, follows God as our ultimate exemplar. Similar to Paul's directive to "follow me as I follow Christ" (1 Corinthians 11:1), working with others allows us to tap into the militant DNA of the body of Christ that was always meant to be present. We were designed to fight alongside others, with access to reinforcements, on a shared mission guided by the apostolic mandate of the Great Commission. In whatever challenges you face, avoid isolating yourself, resist putting yourself on an island, and ensure you remain connected with the people who are meant to support you in your journey.

A crucial point to conclude this section is: don't allow your past experiences to isolate you from the divine destiny God has for you. It's common to let painful interactions shape the way we approach relationships. Instead of viewing people through the lens Christ intended, we often see them through the filter of past hurts. Remember, God has reinforcements lined up for you—a group of people to join you in the battle and support you along this journey.

## Armor of God

*Finally, my brothers, be strong in the Lord and in the power of His might. Put on the whole armor of God that you may be able to stand against the schemes of the devil. For our fight is not against flesh and blood, but against principalities, against powers, against the rulers of the darkness of this world, and against spiritual forces of evil in the heavenly places. Therefore take up the whole armor of God that you may be able to resist in the evil day, and having done all, to stand. Stand therefore, having your waist girded with truth, having put on the breastplate of righteousness, having your feet*

*fitted with the readiness of the gospel of peace, and above all, taking the shield of faith, with which you will be able to extinguish all the fiery arrows of the evil one. Take the helmet of salvation and the sword of the Spirit, which is the word of God.*
Ephesians 6:10-17

When we envision armor, it's often associated with attire designed for defense in warfare. Historically, armor shielded individuals from harm, particularly during times when weapons like blades were crafted from iron, steel, and other metals. Similarly, the armor of God functions as a protective covering for various parts of our being, safeguarding us from harm. Each piece serves the purpose of defending different aspects of our physical and spiritual selves.

The verse instructs us to have our waist girded with truth, also referred to in some versions as the belt of truth. When considering the function of a belt in an outfit, it holds the entire ensemble together, supporting every piece between the legs and the torso. Similarly, we as believers must always make truth a standard. When our waist is girded with truth, we allow this truth to keep everything together in the way we move, how we posture ourselves, and how we live our lives.

The passage then mentions the breastplate of righteousness, which safeguards the chest and torso. It illustrates how our conduct and the way we carry ourselves, moving towards righteousness, can serve as a form of protection. By aligning ourselves with righteousness, we tap into its power and safeguard ourselves, not striving toward our own righteousness but rather God's righteousness (see Matthew 6:33). Recognizing that righteousness is a form of protection, it not only safeguards our reputation but also shields our heart. The breastplate is a primary protector of the heart, and when we stand in the righteousness of God, our heart is more effectively shielded.

Having your feet fitted with the readiness of the gospel of peace not only safeguards our spiritual movement but also provides a solid foundation for navigating and overcoming the terrain ahead. Athletes and military personnel alike emphasize the importance of proper footwear. The choice and fit of what you wear on your feet can be crucial. When we ready our feet with the gospel of peace, we move in alignment with the gospel and stand in His peace, regardless of the challenges in the terrain.

One of the most powerful illustrations in this armor is the shield of faith. The passage emphasizes that the shield of faith has the power to extinguish every fiery arrow of the evil one. Fiery arrows were a common war tactic in ancient times, so understanding the capability to block and completely extinguish those arrows is significant. This highlights the fact that faith serves as our protection; faith has the power to block and extinguish every fiery dart of the enemy. When we are firmly grounded in our identity as sons, we can confidently lift our faith and wield it against every attack.

The scripture then discusses the helmet of salvation, arguably one of the most important pieces of armor, protecting our minds. It's intriguing that our very salvation is illustrated as the safeguard for our minds. The mind holds great importance; Scripture emphasizes our transformation through the renewing of our minds (Romans 12:2). However, after this mental transformation, we need to protect and uphold that change. Our salvation establishes a standard in our lives, urging us to elevate everything we expose ourselves to. We no longer settle for entertainment that is morally questionable, and we set a standard in that area. We are cautious about the influences around us, understanding that, while we are called to love everybody, our inner circle, much like Jesus, should consist of those who align with our purpose. Being anchored in our salvation protects our minds from the influences that the enemy and the world attempt to impose.

I conclude in the same place we started because the armor description in Ephesians ends with the sword of the Spirit, which is the word of God. When we understand that defensive measures are necessary to guard ourselves, we can then engage in warfare without leaving ourselves vulnerable. While these aspects are spiritual, and we can pray on spiritual armor, it's crucial to live them out so that we can genuinely say that we wear this armor.

# Worship

*So, they rose up early in the morning and went out to the Wilderness of Tekoa. And when they went out, Jehoshaphat stood and said, "Listen to me, Judah and those dwelling in Jerusalem. Believe in the Lord your God, and you will be supported. Believe His prophets, and you will succeed." And he consulted with the people and then appointed singers for the Lord and those praising Him in holy attire as they went before those equipped for battle, saying, "Praise the Lord, for His mercy endures forever." When they began singing and praising, the Lord set ambushes against Ammon, Moab, and Mount Seir, who had come against Judah; and they were defeated. Then the Ammonites and Moabites stood up against those dwelling in Mount Seir to destroy and finish them. Then when they made an end of the inhabitants of Seir, each man attacked his companion to destroy each other. And Judah came to the watchtower of the wilderness, and they turned to the vast army and saw only corpses lying on the ground. No one was spared.*

2 Chronicles 20:20-24

Jehoshaphat secured victory by engaging in worship before the battle, moving in the faith that the battle belonged to the Lord. Worship is not only a means to connect with God, although it serves that purpose. Worship is also a weapon against the forces of evil, capable of changing atmospheres and transforming everything it touches.

Worship extends beyond a moment of singing praises with beautiful music played by minstrels; it is a lifestyle that involves living for God and continually consecrating your walk. This is why we consider giving as a form of worship—when we sacrificially give financially, we offer worship to the Lord with our finances. In this passage, as they marched towards the battle against three different nations—a situation that seemed to spell defeat for the armies of Israel—their victory was secured. They achieved this by placing the team responsible for worship and praise ahead of the army, prioritizing worship before the fight. Imagine how every battle and obstacle would change if we put our worship before our fight.

Too often, as a pastor, I've observed people getting so entangled in their situations that they overlook worship. This happens partly because individuals tend to minimize worship, associating it only with something that occurs on Sundays before a sermon or during a worship service. However, when we embrace lifestyles of worship, we can enter a different realm of victory in warfare. By prioritizing worship, we place God before us—before our worries and frustrations—and allow Him to be worshipped and praised, regardless of the warfare we face.

*At midnight Paul and Silas were praying and singing hymns to God, and the prisoners were listening to them. Suddenly there was a great earthquake, so that the foundations of the prison were shaken. And immediately all the doors were opened and everyone's shackles were loosened.*

Acts 16:25-26

Paul and Silas, even in their circumstances of being locked up in prison, chose to continuously worship and praise. It's essential for us to learn that whether we are stuck in a challenging place or fighting a battle, praising and worshiping the Lord is crucial because worship serves as a weapon against the forces of evil. In this passage, we witness that worship literally creates a seismic shift, breaking open the earth and the shackles that bound them. Worship has the power to open doors and break bondage. When we grasp this reality and begin to live lives of worship, we can experience the breakthrough and victory meant for us as believers.

# 5

# An Inheritance of Victory

As believers, victory is not something we fight for but rather a place we fight from. What do I mean? The answer is simple. We are already promised victory, and that is the position and posture from which we engage in the battle. Instead of fighting from uncertain places, we should fight from a position of certain victory.

*The Lord gave Israel all the land that He swore to give to their fathers. They took possession of it and lived in it. The Lord gave them rest all around, according to all that He swore to their fathers. Not a man among their enemies stood before them, and the Lord delivered all their enemies into their hands. Not a single word of all the good things that the Lord had spoken to the children of Israel failed. They all came to pass.*
Joshua 21:43-45

Just as the Israelites had an inheritance of the promised land—a land given to them as God's chosen people—we often forget that we are not bound by our circumstances but destined to live in the promise. Even if the manifestation hasn't occurred yet, it is prophetically on the way. So, for whatever promise God has given, we should not underestimate His ability to fulfill that promise.

Joshua is a great example for anyone seeking to grow their faith in what God has promised. Mentored by Moses himself, Joshua began as a spy scouting the promised land. He and Caleb were the only two with the faith to declare that they could conquer it. Eventually becoming the general and leader of the Israelite nation, Joshua answered the same call as Moses but with unwavering obedience. His ability to hear God and obey teaches us valuable lessons. The passage highlights a powerful statement: "not a man of their enemies stood before them." Not one person could hinder their conquest because God had spoken the promise of victory over them. Victory was already declared, ensuring its manifestation. When we understand that God's plan for us is predestined for manifestation, no amount of warfare can thwart it. We fight from victory because victory is promised.

Some legalistic individuals may argue that this promise was made to the Israelites, part of a covenant with a different group of people. However, I would assert that our covenant and inheritance come through Jesus Christ as Christians. As believers, we access all of God's promises through sonship, which is anchored by our salvation given to us through the perfect sacrifice of the Lamb. Most reading this book should know this. Therefore, when we comprehend that our inheritance comes from Christ, we also understand that our victory comes from Christ.

*But thanks be to God, who gives us the victory through our Lord Jesus Christ!*
1 Corinthians 15:57

The passage declares that victory has been given to us through Christ. Understanding this is crucial in the context of spiritual warfare. Too often, I've observed the body of Christ appearing more like punching bags than warriors. While I recognize that this stems from identity crises and pain, I strongly believe it's time for us to step into our true identity as those promised victory from the Most High.

*Who shall separate us from the love of Christ? Shall tribulation, or distress, or persecution, or famine, or nakedness, or peril, or sword? As it is written: "For Your sake we are killed all day long; we are counted as sheep for the slaughter." No, in all these things we are more than conquerors through Him who loved us. For I am persuaded that neither death nor life, neither angels nor principalities nor powers, neither things present nor things to come, neither height nor depth, nor any other created thing, shall be able to separate us from the love of God, which is in Christ Jesus our Lord.*
Romans 8:35-39

The passage affirms that we are more than conquerors in tribulation, distress, persecution, famine, nakedness, peril, or the sword. If we're honest with ourselves, how often have we succumbed to seasons of distress or peril, becoming subjects to circumstances rather than victors of our own stories? After declaring that we are more than conquerors, the passage extends this victory to a deeper level, encompassing life, death, and even angels and principalities. This speaks to the inherited victory that marks our lives. If we have victory over beings not of this world, why would we be moved by anything else? If, through Christ, we are more than conquerors over life and death, what could possibly sway us?

How often have we heard this verse preached in our churches, declaring that we are more than conquerors when everything is going well, yet forgetting this aspect of our identity in the midst of actual conflicts? Understanding our identity as more than conquerors changes the dynamic and terrain of the fight. What does it mean to be a conqueror? In a warfare scenario, it's the person who defeats the other. When engaged in spiritual warfare against powers, principalities, and forces of evil, we realize that we are more than conquerors against all evil. Rooted in this identity, we grasp that victory is already ours. Now, it's up to us to wage good warfare. While we've discussed various tactics and weapons for our warfare, using them must come from a place of certainty that they will be effective in our hands. Scripture states, "the weapons of our warfare" (2 Corinthians 10:4). While the battle belongs to the Lord (2 Chronicles 20:15), it's our warfare to fight.

*For whoever is born of God overcomes the world, and the victory that overcomes the world is our faith.*
1 John 5:4

God has given us victory over the world through our faith. As we discussed earlier, understanding the power of the shield of faith is crucial. When your faith truly lies in Christ, and you bring yourself into real sonship, you can overcome every obstacle of the world. We do not change or overcome sin, temptation, and any other worldly obstacle on our own. Rather, our faith in God gives us the strength and ability to overcome. After all, Scripture says that He has given us everything we need to live a godly life through knowing Him (2 Peter 1:3 NLT).

> *Then I saw the beast and the kings of the earth with their armies gathered to wage war against Him who sat on the horse and against His army. But the beast was captured and with him the false prophet who worked signs in his presence, by which he deceived those who received the mark of the beast and those who worshipped his image. These two were thrown alive into the lake of fire that burns with brimstone. The remnant were slain with the sword which proceeded out of the mouth of Him who sat on the horse. And all the birds gorged themselves with their flesh.*
> Revelation 19:19-21

As believers, we inherit a victory that has already been written. When the enemy attempts to wage war against Jesus, he always loses. As heirs with Christ (Romans 8:17), we share in this prophetic image of the end times. It envisions a moment when the Antichrist and all the armies of darkness are defeated by Christ and the army of light. Our victory is assured. It is already written in the Word, which God holds above His own name, that we have the victory. While this truth echoes in the context of the end times, we also have victory in every aspect of our walk—overcoming every obstacle, defeating every enemy, and triumphing over all the warfare we face.

Embrace your identity as someone "made for war" and recognize that you are an inheritor of victory. When you fight from this inheritance and posture yourself in this victory, your prophetic destiny will manifest within the warfare you face.

## From Generational Curses to Generational Blessings

In the realm of spiritual warfare and deliverance, the term "Generational Curse" is a familiar concept within the church. Whether individuals have assisted someone in breaking such a curse or have personally overcome one, this notion has made its way into the fabric of the church. Essentially, a Generational Curse can be recognized by recurring afflictions within a specific bloodline. This might manifest as a cycle of broken relationships through divorce or a pattern of sickness leading to early death. As believers, we are called to be "Bloodline Breakers," disrupting these destructive cycles through repentance and prayers of deliverance. God remains faithful in delivering us as we draw near to Him and surrender every aspect of our lives, including breaking Generational Curses.

*You shall not bow down to them or serve them; for I, the Lord your God, am a jealous God, visiting the iniquity of the fathers on the children to the third and fourth generation of those who hate Me.*
Exodus 20:5

You won't find this verse adorning many Christian kitchen mugs, as it's one of the more challenging passages that some people tend to avoid. However, despite its difficulty, the intent of this verse was never to instill fear. The punishment mentioned in the verse stemmed from idolatry and a lack of reverence, leading to the imposition of a Generational Curse.

Not every sin will result in a Generational Curse for you or your family. These curses typically arise from severe and deliberate sins that go unrepented. For additional insights on Generational Curses, you can explore Alexander Pagani's book titled *The Secrets to Generational Curses*. Believers must grasp the significance of confessing to God and one another, as well as practicing repentance. These actions not only maintain close communication with God and foster humility among fellow believers but also keep us spiritually aligned, away from our sins and the sins of our ancestors.

As inheritors of victory, Generational Curses are not part of our inheritance. Embracing our full identity in spiritual warfare as Sons and Daughters allows us to recognize that the seeds of righteousness and faithfulness we plant can lead to Generational Blessings. While the church has long acknowledged the concept of Generational Curses, it's equally important to recognize the existence of Generational Blessings. Just as we aim to accumulate financial wealth for our children, we should also aspire to be a source of generational blessing within our bloodline.

*Now it will be, if you diligently obey the voice of the Lord your God, being careful to do all His commandments which I am commanding you today, then the Lord your God will set you high above all the nations of the earth. And all these blessings will come on you and overtake you if you listen to the voice of the Lord your God. You will be blessed in the city and blessed in the field. Your offspring will be blessed, and the produce of your ground, and the offspring of your livestock, the increase of your herd and the flocks of your sheep.*
Deuteronomy 28:1-4

This passage emphasizes that by listening to the commands of the Lord and obeying Him, blessings will come upon you, extending to your offspring. Choosing a cycle of obedience and blessing rather than one of sin and curses allows you to positively impact the landscape for future generations. It's essential to recognize that while leaving a financial and moral inheritance is important, leaving an inheritance of obedience, favor, and blessing is equally crucial.

God desires to establish a standard in our families, and it begins with us. Our understanding transforms everything. You might wonder how this connects to warfare. This book not only guides us in waging effective warfare but also reveals it as part of our inheritance as sons and daughters of the Most High. Many of us grapple with battles within broken cycles prevailing in our families. It's time to instill a culture of repentance and obedience, bringing about a profound shift from cycles of curses to cycles of favor and blessing in our families and homes.

I'm prompted to address this because, in our spiritual battles and in interceding for others, we must be careful not to set ourselves up for unnecessary warfare. Weeding out generational cycles can help us clear the battlefield, preparing us for what is truly meant for us. By embracing a culture of faithfulness, confession, and repentance, we position ourselves in a place where victory is imminent, guided by biblical principles, the Holy Spirit, and the purpose that He has chosen us for.

## It's Time to Change your Posture.

We can't truly experience the victory meant for us until we break free from our current state. One crucial step is changing our posture—the position we hold in the midst of warfare. How are we aligning ourselves with the identity God has bestowed upon us, being "Made for War"? It's time to shift from a defensive stance to becoming an offensive weapon against the enemy. Rather than merely patching up after attacks, we should embrace our identity, wield the weapons of our warfare, and conquer the legal rights the enemy has held over us. This shift in placement and posture not only promises victory but makes it irrefutable.

In the realm of spiritual warfare, positioning oneself may lead to an identity crisis when there's a lack of understanding about where God has placed us. This uncertainty can impact how we perceive ourselves.

*Even when we were dead in sins, made us alive together with Christ (by grace you have been saved), and He raised us up and seated us together in the heavenly places in Christ Jesus.*
Ephesians 2:5-6

Recall our discussion on the victorious nature of our inheritance—this passage emphasizes that in Christ, we are destined to be seated in heavenly places. It's profound to grasp that we're not merely esteemed but elevated in the Spiritual Realm, granted authority and elevation by His grace and love. Going deeper, this signifies the extent of our inheritance and how it gives us divine access against the kingdom of darkness. Positioned in Heavenly Realms, we need not engage in earthly struggles but wield authority to wage war and declare the manifestation of the Lord's will.

Some individuals might be surprised by the self-perception of certain Christians, often underestimating their inherent value and power. Some believers may think God loves them only because the preacher says so, without truly grasping the depth of His love for them and their position in inheritance. One crucial lesson I've learned is not only to understand your value or how God values you but also to recognize how intricately you were made. Regardless of challenges or circumstances, God's opinion of you and His perception remain unwavering. Thus, the power you carry, and the inheritance destined for you do not change. As scripture declares, "For I am the Lord, I do not change" (Malachi 3:6). God has not altered His stance on what He has spoken about you in the Spiritual Realm. In the face of any adversity, don't let the enemy strip you of your identity.

Given this, how can we alter our posture? Knowing that we are seated in heavenly places and acknowledging that our identity must be firmly rooted in God, it implies our stance should be in Christ, fully aware of how it has positioned us. This not only anchors your identity, providing stability against any attack, but also grants empowerment from where your supernatural access originates.

*For this reason I bow my knees to the Father of our Lord Jesus Christ, from whom the whole family in heaven and earth is named.*

Ephesians 3:14-15

Understanding how we position ourselves involves recognizing the perpetual need for reverence. We must navigate in the fear of the Lord, adopting a posture of bowing. The passage affirms, *"For this reason, I bow,"* suggesting a stance that allows us to move accordingly. When we bow, it signifies not only our submission to the Lord but also a deliberate pause in our hectic pace, enabling us to bow before Him. This act requires us to cast aside distractions, fears, frustrations, and various other hindrances, assuming a posture of reverence and awe for the Lord.

Acknowledging our identity and divine placement as those seated in heavenly places is crucial, but we must also recognize that reverence holds a key position in spiritual warfare. When we assume a posture of surrender and reverence for God, transformative shifts occur. Consider Jehoshaphat and the Israelite army, demonstrating reverence by placing worship before their fighters, and the breakthrough manifested on the other side. Victory awaits on the other side of reverential acts. Amidst our warfare, we should contemplate what reverential actions we can take, how we can better posture ourselves in reverence, and bow before the Lord.

A crucial aspect to consider in positioning ourselves for success in spiritual warfare is our proximity to the Lord. Power lies in how closely we draw ourselves to Him. Our God is relational, emphasizing closeness and intimacy rather than distance or separation. Within our relationship with God, we discover not only the security of His love but also a solid foundation for our identity in warfare and the power inherent in our inheritance.

As we draw near to God and experience His closer presence, a purification process unfolds, as written in James 4:8, *"Draw near to God, and He will draw near to you. Cleanse your hands, you sinners, and purify your hearts, you double-minded."* This proximity initiates a transformative journey, leading to a deeper level of repentance and genuine change. This becomes significant in our preparation for spiritual warfare, as transformation through repentance and the power of God's presence equip us for battle and ready us to live out the powerful words we proclaim.

The potential for boundless power unfolds when we draw near to God and cultivate our relationship with Him. Scripture, as in 2 Peter 1:3, affirms, *"His divine power has given to us all things that pertain to life and godliness through the knowledge of Him who has called us by His own glory and excellence."* In other translations, it is expressed that through His divine power, we have everything needed for a godly life through knowing Him. Consider this: all that is essential for living a godly life is discovered in our relationship with Him, requiring our intentional closeness to God. Submission to Him is vital, as the scripture instructs, *"Submit to God, resist the devil, and he will flee."* The synergy of power and submission is intricately tied to our relationship, reverence, and the act of drawing near to God. Reflecting on Peter's authority over demons even by his passing shadow, it becomes evident that such authority stems from the depth of his relationship with Jesus and his proximity to God.

*"He said to them, "Do not be frightened. You are looking for Jesus of*

*Nazareth, who was crucified. He is risen. He is not here. See the place where they laid Him."*
Mark 16:6

A foundational truth for believers transcends any book or entity: Jesus has already triumphed in the greatest battle. He obliterated sin and death, providing us the opportunity to lead godly lives, experience salvation, and live as His new creations. As we highlighted earlier, being heirs with Christ grants us access to a victory that frees us from being subjected to loss, defeat, or any other form of destruction. Instead, we become vessels of victory, bestowed with this inheritance through Christ.

As believers, we are destined for spiritual warfare—overcoming and dismantling the legal rights and even the illegal rights of the enemy that have kept us bound in cycles. Engaged in this spiritual battle, we are not left defenseless. On the contrary, we are equipped, dangerous, and inheritors of victory. My aspiration is that, through reading this book, you transition from being a mere bystander or collateral damage in the war between the kingdom of light and darkness. Instead, envision an active role as a warrior, a role for which you were inherently made. No longer passive in the face of Satan's abuse, we rise as those who engage in noble warfare against the kingdom of darkness. God, in His promises and declarations of our identity, designates us as victors, inherently made for war from birth in our spiritual DNA. May these truths empower you to embrace your destined role and actively partake in the victory secured for you.

Remember, your inheritance is one of victory, for you are inherently "Made for War," enlisted as a member of God's special forces against the armies of darkness. You are the one whom God will train for battle and warfare, providing everything needed to live it out. Embrace this divine calling and live in the fullness of your spiritual DNA as one who is Made for War.

## Final Revelation

As believers made for war, we must remember what has been said here. It is not enough to simply accept that warfare is part of our identity; we must begin the process of engaging in this spiritual battle. This involves removing any legal rights the enemy has tried to hold over us and moving into deeper realms of freedom. We achieve this by walking in forgiveness, avoiding harboring secrets or lies, breaking and separating ourselves from any soul ties, and absolutely keeping away from and breaking any demonic agreements that might exist in our lives.

We must acknowledge that this is a spiritual war, and although we walk in the flesh, we do not wage war according to the flesh (2 Corinthians 10:3). By understanding this, we can grasp a greater revelation: we are given authority on the battlefield and in the courts as those made for war. We are wired for victory, serving both as Warriors and Judicial Enforcers. We stand in the gap as Defense Attorneys for others, helping them through different levels of healing and deliverance, while also prosecuting the forces of darkness.

We must recognize that we are armed and dangerous, a threat against the kingdom of darkness. Our threat increases as we equip ourselves with prayer, fasting, prophecy, calling in reinforcements, the armor of God, and worship. By doing so, we truly become God's nuclear weapon against the forces of the enemy.

Growing in this realm allows us to encounter the inheritance already prepared for us—an inheritance of victory. We know that every promise from God far outweighs any problem from the enemy. As we walk toward our calling, we can bring our families from places of Generational Curses to Generational Blessings. It is time to change our posture to that of victors who live in the fullness of their inheritance. When we acknowledge that we are Made for War, we no longer move from a place of fear or inadequacy but rather thrive from a place of mastery.

www.ingramcontent.com/pod-product-compliance
Lightning Source LLC
Chambersburg PA
CBHW051700090426
42736CB00013B/2465